DEEP LEARNING

Fundamentals of Deep Learning for Beginners

TABLE OF CONTENTS

Chapter 1

Introduction to Deep Learning

Let's review some concepts of machine learning

If I asked you about machine learning, you'll probably imagine a robot or something like the Terminator. But in fact, machine learning is not only involved in robotics but also in several other applications.

You can also imagine something like a spam filter as one of the very first applications in machine learning that has improved millions of people lives. In this chapter, I will introduce you to what machine learning is and how it works.

Machine learning is the field of programming where computers can learn from data. In the above example, the program can easily know if the emails are important or not, aka spam. In machine learning, the data is called a training set or examples.

Machine Learning

Let's assume that you would like to write the filter program without using machine learning methods. In this case, you will do the following steps:

· In the beginning, you will need to know what this program is. You may select them for its sentences that include something like "win," "millions," and so on.

· Second, if you want to implement an algorithm to find any form of these problems, and then the software can exactly find these forms emails as spam if it found many forms before, then it will be able to find it easily

· Finally, you will go to check your software, and then do the first two steps over again to make sure that it works well.

Because the program is not complex software, it contains a very long list of rules that are not easy to maintain. But when developing that same software using machine learning (ML), it will be maintainable.

Additionally, when you receive an email, senders change their emails that contain words like "any word" or "for you" because all of their emails have been detected as a spam in the past. The program with traditional techniques would need to be updated, and that means if there are any other changes you will also need to update your code again and forever.

On the other hand, the program that uses ML techniques will automatically detect this change by users, and it will flag them without you.

Also, we can use machine learning to solve problems that are very complex for non-Machine Learning software. Take speech recognition for example: when you say "one" or "two," the program should be able to distinguish the difference. So you will need to write an algorithm that measures sound in order to complete this task.

In the end, machine learning will help us to learn, and its algorithms can see what we have learned.

When should you use machine learning?

• When you face a problem that requires a lot of long lists of rules to get a solution, machine learning techniques can simplify your code so you can achieve better performance.

• Very complex problems for which there is no solution when using the traditional approach.

• Non- stable environments: machine learning software can adapt to new data

MLoptions

The algorithms of this subject can be divided into categories depending on:

• If they need us to work and learn:

- Supervised

- Unsupervised

- Semi-supervised

- Reinforcement Learning

  • If they will not need us to work.

  • If they work with this kind of inputs and refer to know this input or can find new forms in the input and then build a solution.

Supervised and unsupervised learning

We can categorize these kind of algorithms and divide them into the following:

- Supervised Learning

- Unsupervised Learning

- Semi-supervised Learning

- Reinforcement Learning

Supervised Learning

Using this type of ML you will need the data that you enter into the software with the problem solving algorithm, called labels.

You should keep in mind that some regression algorithms can be used for classifications and vice versa.

The most important supervised algorithms

- K-Nears Neighbors

- Linear Regression

- Neural Networks

- Support Vector Machines

- Logistic Regression

\-   Decision Trees and Random Forests

Unsupervised Learning

With this type of ML, you can guess that the data is unlabeled.

The most important unsupervised algorithms:

Clustering: k-means, Hierarchical Cluster Analysis

Association rule learning: Eclat, Apriori

Visualization and dimensionality reduction: Kernel PCA, t-distributed, PCA

To give you an example, if you have lots of data on your website visitors and are using one of our algorithms for detection of groups with similar visitors, it may find that 65% of the visitors are males who love watching movies in the evening, while 30% are watching plays in the evening.

In this case, when using a clustering algorithm it will divide every group into smaller ones.

Intro to deep learning

You can see around us, the development of the new hardware and computing platforms due to the new trends like big data and so on. So as a result, there is more demand for better products and also enterprises seeking to leverage their resources in an effective way to meet these requirements. At this point, they need new technologies like machine and deep learning.

As we all know that machine learning is the science of making computers that has the ability to learn without being programmed explicitly, deep learning on the other hand is a subset of machine learning that is used to understand multiple levels of the data representation.

In other words, this technique not only has predictive and classification ability but it can also learn a different level of complex data.

Deep Learning Models

Let's talk now about the models of deep learning, it will be very useful to start discussing the models of deep learning.

You will need some basics of mathematics and statistics to understand the following content. Let's talk about the first model; the single layer perceptron model, or SLP.

Single Layer Perceptron Model (SLP)

In this model, you will find out that it is a very simple form of neural networks and also the foundation for the more sophisticated models that have been developed in this field.

Usually, we use this simple model in classification problems where we need to give the data something called "labels" (it may be binary or multinomial, depending on the input). These values in your input layers will be sent to the output layer after the multiplication by weights, and a bias will be added to the total sum.

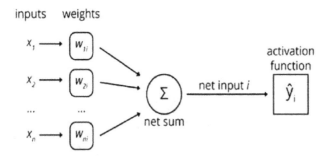

Multilayer Perceptron Model (MLP)

The multilayer perceptron model has many layers that are interconnected in such a way that they will make a feed-forward neural network. Every neuron in each layer has a direct connection, or more connections, to the neurons of a separate layer.

One of the most important things to distinguish that are the many factors in the multilayer model and the other model is the back-propagation.

The back propagation is a common methodology that shows us how to train a neural network.

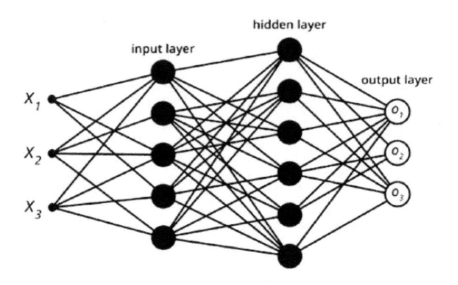

Convolutional Neural Networks (CNNs)

CNNs, or convolutional neural networks, are just models which are the most popular models that are used for computer vision and image processing applications.

Actually, they are developed to mimic the structure of the visual cortex in animals. Convolutional neural networks have the neurons arranged in three dimensions (depth, height, width).

The neurons in any layer are just only connected to a very small part of the prior layer. Convolutional neural networks models are the best models for computer vision and image processing apps.

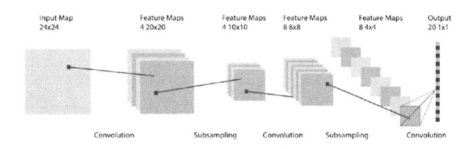

Recurrent Neural Networks (RNNs)

This kind of model is of an artificial neural network, or ANN, where the connections between units form a cycle. A directed cycle is just a sequence with vertices and also edges. You can see this model used for speech and handwriting recognition.

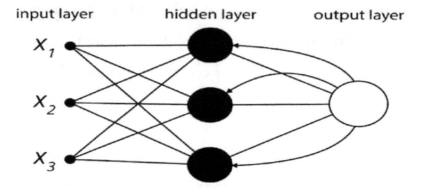

Deep Belief Networks (DBNs)

This kind of model is similar to the Restricted Boltzmann Machines as you can see in the figure below. It has every subnetwork of every hidden layer. They are generally a model of multilayers.

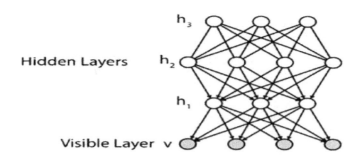

Questions

1. What is deep learning?

2. Can you explain the difference between the different deep learning models?

Chapter 2

Mathematics for Deep Learning

Statistics is the core concept behind deep learning and if you want to know what deep learning is, Statistics is essential. Generally speaking, statistics functions by analyzing data and the end goal is to take certain actions on the basis of what has been analyzed.

This does not however in any way mean that statistics and deep learning are the same thing or even in the same field. Statistics is simply the concept you have to familiarize yourself with if you want to get into the machine learning and artificial intelligence field.

Statistical Concepts

Before we even start discussing machine learning and statistics, there is another concept that is very important to understand – probability.

Probability in simple terms is to measure through different means and yardsticks the occurrence of an event. Machine learning is made up of many models which have to be deterministic and based on certain regulations, just like the concepts of probability are related to algorithms to the expectation and maximize algorithm in ML. Furthermore, many of the algorithms in deep learning models and architecture are complex, for example, a neural network that keeps repeating itself and CNNs. In mathematics, we like to define these as:

Probability of Event A, number of times event A occurs, and all possible events

This is what we use to determine what the probability is of the most frequent of occurrences, and except this, there are other ways you can use to determine the Bayesian. The basis of this theory is made up of certain assumptions – that is "conditional probability." If we look at this from another side, we see that the probability of any event is easily impacted by the kind of conditions that exist in the status-quo and even by the events that happened before.

We can define the conditional probability with this next formula.

The definition of the conditional probability can be like this next formula. The probability of A, if we have B given, is equal to the following:

$P(A \mid B) = P(A \cap B)/P(B)$

$P(A \mid B) = P(A)$

$P(B \mid A) = P(B)$

$P(A \cap B) = P(B)\, P(A)$

The given image shows to you A and B sets. As you can see, the union of A and B happens like the two circles overlapping.

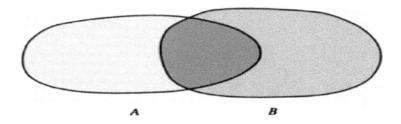

This equation can't really be true in any given circumstance, because we know A and B events are dependent.

"And" & "Or"

When we are working with probability – for example, if we take two events A & B and try to evaluate them – the probability that A occurs can be described using this statement – "The probability of A *& B*," or "The probability of A *or* B. You can say *or* to denote the sum of probable events, whereas *and* implies the product of probabilities of the event."

The following are the equations needed:

And (multiplicative law of probability) is the probability of the intersection of two
events A and B:

$$P(A \cap B) = P(A)\, P(B|A)$$

If the events are independent, then

$$P(A \cap B) = P(A)\, P(B)$$

or (additive law of probability) is the probability of the union of two events A and B:

$$P(A \cup B) = P(A) + P(B) - P(A \cap B)$$

The symbol means $P(A \cup B)$ "the probability of A or B."

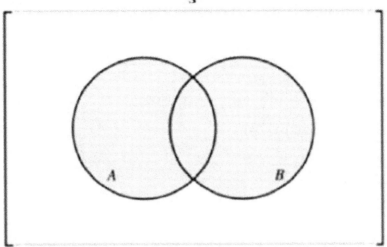

The probability of the two different events A and B occurring is represented by their respective circles and these circles do not overlap when the probability of A or B will be calculated by adding the two parts with the intersection.

For example, S or Z can be taken as the addition of all groups that we take in any problem, and add to this the space which is exterior to the sets. The probability of S will now be 1.

As is evident, the area that is outside of A and B is representative of the probability of the opposite events to them occurring. For example, let's say that A and B represent the assumption of a father coming home by 7pm. and a mother coming home at 7 p.m., in that sequence.

The white area would then be the probability of neither of them coming home by 7pm.

Bayes' Theorem

As mentioned before, the Bayesian rule has started to get a lot of positive feedback within the circles of artificial intelligence and deep learning. There is a drawback to these methods since they require a huge amount of hard coding, the power they have is a direct result of a relatively simple theory underpinning them in which having power can be applied to an array of contexts.

This concept has the core concept of conditional probability as its base. Bayes' theorem can simply be said as the concept that assumes that the probability of event A is somehow related to the probability of other such events:

$P(A|B) = P(A)\ P(B|A)P(B)$

Random Variables

A random variable can simply be said as a quantity whose measure and value are directly related to a set of possible random events, with the events being associated with probability. The value of a random variable is known even before it is drawn, but we can also define it as a function that comes from the same area. Except in special circumstances, we tend to draw random variables through the simple method of random sampling.

Random sampling – Random sampling of say something like a huge population is said to happen when each and every observation is picked in a way that every event is as likely to be picked as all the other events inside that population. When random sampling, there are two kinds of encounters that may occur:

Discrete random variables and *continuous random variables*. The first one is with reference to variables that can only have a limited number of different values, while the second one refers to variables that can have a limitless number of possible variables.

An example of this can be the number of motorbikes in a car parking versus the theoretical change in the percentage change of bond price. When we are trying to analyze these random variables, we tend to use a variety of statistics that readers will see repeated frequently.

For example, arithmetic means are used directly in algorithms such as the K-means clustering while at the same time being a theoretical base of the model evaluation statistics, like the mean squared error (will be mentioned again later in this chapter).

If we just simply look at arithmetic means in the basic form we can define them as the central tendency of a limited set of values – to be more specific, it is the total of all the values which is then divided by the amount of values there were. Arithmetically, this can be defined by the following equation:

$$\bar{x} = \frac{1}{N} \sum_{i=1}^{N} x_i$$

We can represent the *arithmetic* mean by taking the most value from a set or multiple values with random variable. But this simply can't be the only mean that you say when trying to understand a random variable.

The *geometric* mean is the statistic which shows the central tendency of a sequence of numbers, but it can only be calculated by taking the product of these values, and not their total.

This can be used generally if we want to compare with each other two distinct items that occur within a sequence, especially if they have an array of properties as individual items. Geometric mean can be described using the following equation:

$$\left(\prod_{i=1}^{n} x_i \right)^{\frac{1}{n}} = (x_1 * x_2 * \ldots * x_n)^{\frac{1}{n}}$$

If you are someone who is working in these fields, and using time is essential for you, a geometric mean can be helpful when determining the value of change over a certain period of time (years, hours, months and so on).

As is evident by what we have discussed, the center of tendency of any random variable is only one of the means of describing data in statistics. Generally, you should analyze the extent to which the data is away from the most probable value.

Logically speaking, this will help you to get the variance and standard deviation. These two statistics are extremely related to each other, but there are a few important differences. Also, it's important to note that the standard deviation is more likely to be referenced than variance that occurs across multiple fields. When you are trying to address the second difference, it will be harder because variance cannot be easily described visually, plus the units of the variance are also ambiguous. Standard deviation occurs in the units of the random variable being analyzed, and therefore it is simpler to represent visually. As an example, when you are evaluating the effectiveness and efficiency of any machine learning algorithm, you should draw the mean squared error from different epochs. It might also help you to pick sample statistics of such variables so you can also calculate the dispersion of such statistics. Arithmetically, we can define variance and standard deviation as:

Variance

$$\sigma^2 = \frac{\Sigma(X-\mu)^2}{N}$$

$$Var(X) = E\left[\left(X - E([X])\right)^2\right]$$

$$= E[X^2] - 2XE[X] + \left(E[X]\right)^2$$

$$= E\left[X^2\right] - 2E[X]E[X] + \left(E[X]\right)^2$$

$$= E\left[X^2\right] - 2E[X]E[X] + \left(E[X]\right)^2$$

Standard Deviation

$$\sigma = \sqrt{\left(\frac{\sum\limits_{i}^{n}(x_i - \bar{x})^2}{n-1}\right)}$$

It's also essential to remember that covariance is also important if you want to measure the extent to which change in a single feature impacts another. In general, you can write it as the following:

$$cov(X,Y) = \frac{1}{n}\sum_{i=1}^{n}(x_i - \bar{x})(y_i - \bar{y})$$

The field of deep learning has always used state of the art technology and has focused on the sophisticated development of modeling relationships between variables that have non-linear correlations; you can also get many estimators that can be used for easier tasks that need this to be a preliminary assumption.

For example, linear regression needs this to be the basic assumption on which it functions, and there are also many machine learning techniques that can create complex data, and some are better at it than others are.

As an example, this will result in you discussing the correlation coefficient that check the extent to which the variables are linearly similar to the other. In math, we can define this as:

$$correlation = \rho = \frac{1}{n}\sum_{i=1}^{n}\frac{(x_i - \bar{x})(y_i - \bar{y})}{\sqrt{(x_i - \bar{x})^2(y_i - \bar{y})^2}}$$

These coefficients have units which have values that are as high as 1 and as low as -1, while the lower bound that reflects the opposite correlation and the upper bound which reflects the complete correlation.

The coefficient of 0 reflects the absolute lack of any correlation that is statistically speaking. If you wish to analyze and compare different machine learning models, especially the ones that show regression, it generally reflects the coefficient of determination (R squared) and mean squared error (MSE).

You can also imagine that R squared is a measure of how correctly the estimated regression line of the model befits the dispersion of the data.

You can also think, as an example that we can say this statistic is known to everyone as the extent of fitness of any given mode. The mse can be best used to measure the average of what the squared error of the prediction of the dispersion of the observed data is. Sequentially, they can be described in the following way:

Coefficient of Determination (R Squared)

$$R^2 = 1 - \sum_i^n \frac{(\hat{y}_i - y)^2}{(\hat{y}_i - \bar{y})^2}$$

Mean Squared Error (MSE)

$$MSE = \frac{1}{n} \sum_{i=1}^n (y_i - \bar{y})^2$$

When we know what these values are, we can discuss more on this later. Briefly speaking, we generally try to get models that have greater R squared values and at the same time a lesser MSE values than the other estimators that are picked.

Linear Algebra

Linear Algebra is essential to learn deep learning and is used highly in machine learning, software engineering as well as data science. The intention of this is not to be a huge review, but simply to familiarize people with some basic concepts at the least.

Scalars and Vectors

What is a scalar?

A scalar can be said to be any unit of value that only has one kind of property or attribute.
Examples of scalar: speed, volume, mass, temperature

What is a magnitude?

Magnitude. There are many scalars that are also known as vectors; vectors are basically the values that can have both direction as well as magnitude. If we have a multitude of scalars when we have a single given vector, we can say this is the element of vector space. Vector space can be differentiated by the simple fact that it is only the sequence of vectors that can be totaled and whose product can be taken, and these can also have other different numerical operations that can be tested on them. Vectors can also be described as a column vector of n numbers.

On the off chance that you need to comprehend this essential example of a vector, I will portray it as the index value. To make it unmistakable, assume that you have a vector x, at that point x1 alludes to the principal value in vector x. Indeed, you can envision a vector as an entry like a record inside a file cabinet. The values inside this vector are the individual sheets of paper, and the vector itself is the envelope that holds every one of these values.

Properties of Vectors

Vector measurements are regularly signified by $\mathbb{R}n$ or $\mathbb{R}m$ where n and m is the quantity of values inside a given vector. For instance, $x\hat{i} \in 5$ indicates an arrangement of 5 vectors with actual segments.

Even though I have just examined a column vector up until this point, we can likewise have a row vector. A change to transform a column vector into a row vector can likewise be played out, this is known as a transposition. A transposition is a change of a grid/vector X with the end goal that the rows of X are composed as the columns of X T, and that the columns of X are composed as the rows of X T.

Addition

$$d = [d_1, d_2, \ldots, d_n]^T \text{ and } e = [e_1, e_2, \ldots, e_n]^T \text{ where}$$

$$d_n = e_n, \text{ for } i = 1, 2, \ldots, n$$

Therefore, the sum of the vectors is the following:

$$d + e = \left[(d_1 + e_1), (e_2 + d_2), \ldots, (d_n + e_n) \right]^T$$

Subtraction

Given that the assumptions from the past case have not changed, the distinction between vectors d and e would be the accompanying:

$$d - e = \left[(d_1 - e_1), (e_2 - d_2), \ldots, (d_n - e_n) \right]^T$$

Axioms

Let a,b, and x be an arrangement of vectors inside set A, and e and d be scalars in B. The accompanying axiom must hold if something is to be a vector space:

Associative Property

The associative property is related to the way that revising the brackets in a given articulation won't change the end result:

$$x+(a+b)=(x+a)+b$$

Commutative Property

The commutative property relates to the way that changing the arrangement of the operands in a given articulation won't change the end result:

$$A + B = B + A$$

Subspaces

A subspace of a vector space is a nonempty subset that fulfills the necessities for a vector space, particularly with the goal that linear combinations remain in the subspace. This subset is "closed" under addition and scalar duplication. All the more eminently, the zero vector will have a place with each subspace.

For instance, the space that lies between the hyperplanes is created by a support vector regression (a machine learning calculation that I will address later) is an example of a subspace. You can see that in the space that will have the correct values for the response variable.

Matrices

A matrix is likewise an essential and another major idea of linear algebra in our numerical review. Basically, a matrix is a rectangular cluster of numbers, images, or expressions organized in rows and columns. Matrices have an assortment of uses, however, they are particularly and regularly used to store numerical information.

For instance, when performing image recognition with a convolutional neural system, we show the pixels in the photographs as numbers inside a 3-dimensional network, showing the matrix for the red, green, and blue photographs involved in a colored photo.

Normally, we take an individual pixel to have 256 individual qualities, and from this scientific elucidation a generally hard to-comprehend portrayal of information ends up showing. In connection to vectors and scalars, a matrix contains scalars for every individual value and is comprised of row and column vectors.

Matrix Properties

Matrices themselves share a considerable lot of the same rudimentary properties that vectors have by definition since matrices are just a variety of vectors in combination. Be that as it may, there are some key contrasts that are essential, especially concerning matrix multiplication.

For instance, matrix multiplication is a key component in seeing how conventional minimum squares regression functions, and why we would be keen on utilizing gradient descent when performing linear regression.

Questions

1. Describe the following:

   Random variables

   Random sampling

   Discrete random variables and continuous random variables.

Chapter 3

Single and Multilayer Perceptron Models

Single Layer Perceptron (SLP) Model

SLP is one of the simplest of the neural network models, and it was developed by scientists McCulloch and Pitts. In the mind of many machine learning developers, SLP is represented as the beginning of artificial intelligence and it provided inspiration for developing other neural network models and machine learning models. The SLP architecture is such that a single neuron is

connected by many synapses, each of which contains a weight.

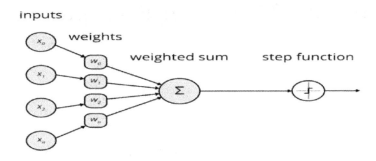

Training the Perceptron Model

We begin the training process by initializing all the weights with values sampled

randomly from a normal distribution. We can use a gradient descent method to train the model, with the objective to minimize the error function.

Limitations of Single Perceptron Models

The main limitation of the SLP models that led to the development of subsequent neural network models is that perceptron models are only accurate when working with data that is clearly linearly separable.

This obviously becomes difficult in situations with much more dense and complex data, and it effectively eliminates this technique's usefulness from classification problems that we would encounter in a practical context.

An example of this is the XOR problem. You can suppose that you have two inputs, $x1$ and $x2$ for which a response, y, is given, then the following is true:

	x_1	$x_2 y$
0	0	0
1	0	1
0	1	1
1	1	0

Now it's time to check out an example using SLP with data that is not rigidly linearly separable to get an understanding of how this model performs. For this example, I've created a simple example function of a single layer perceptron model.

For the error function I used 1 minus the AUC score, as this would give us a numerical quantity so that we could train the weight matrix via back-propagation using gradient descent.

You should feel free to use the next function as well as change the arguments.

You should start with setting some of the same parameters that we did with respect to our linear regression algorithm performed via gradient descent, if you need to review the specifics of the gradient descent and how it's applied for parameter updating.

The only difference here is that we're using a different error function than the mean squared error used in regression:

```
singleLayerPerceptron<- function(x = x_train, y = y_train,
max_iter = 1000, tol = .001){
#Initializing weights and other parameters
weights <- matrix(rnorm(ncol(x_train)))
x <- as.matrix(x_train)
cost <- 0
iter<- 1
converged <- FALSE
```

Here, we define a function for a single layer perceptron, setting parameters similar to that of the linear regression via the defined gradient decent algorithm. As always, we cross-validate (this section of code redacted, please check GitHub) our data upon each iteration to prevent the weights from overfitting. In the following code, we define the algorithm for the SLP described in the preceding section:

```
while(converged == FALSE){
#Our Log Odds Threshold here is the Average Log Odds
weighted_sum<- 1/(1 + exp(-(x%*%weights)))
y_h<- ifelse(weighted_sum<= mean(weighted_sum), 1, 0)
error <- 1 - roc(as.factor(y_h), y_train)$auc
}
```

In the end, you will train our algorithm using gradient descent with the error defined as $1 - AUC$.

In this code, you will write the processes that we repeat until we converge upon an optimal solution or the maximum number of iterations allowed:

```r
#Weight Updates using Gradient Descent
#Error Statistic := 1 - AUC
if (abs(cost - error) >tol | iter<max_iter){
cost <- error
iter<- iter + 1
gradient <- matrix(ncol = ncol(weights), nrow =
nrow(weights))
for(i in 1:nrow(gradient)){
gradient[i,1] <- (1/length(y_h))*(0.01*error)*(weights[i,1])
}
```

(Next section redacted, please check github!)

As always, it's very important for developers to evaluate the results of their experiment. This shows the AUC score summary statistics in addition to the last AUC score with its respective ROC curve plotted:


```r
#Performance Statistics
cat("The AUC of the Trained Model is ", roc(as.factor(y_h),
y_train)$auc)
cat("\nTotal number of iterations: ", iter)
curve <- roc(as.factor(y_h), y_train)
plot(curve, main = "ROC Curve for Single Layer
```

Perceptron")

}

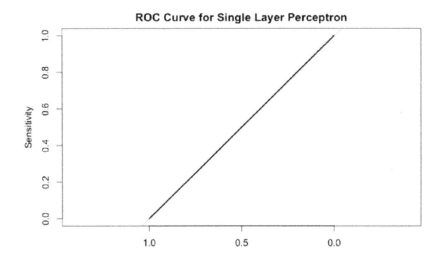

Multi-Layer Perceptron (MLP) Model

Multi layer models are distinguished from SLPs by the action when there are hidden layers that affect the output of the model. This distinguishing factor also happens to be their strength because it better allows them to handle XOR issues. Every neuron in this model receives an input from a neuron—or from the environment in the case of the input neuron.

Each neuron is connected by a synapse, attached to which is a weight similar to the SLP. Upon introducing one hidden layer, we can have the model represent a Boolean function,

47

and introducing two layers allows the network to represent an arbitrary decision space.

If we move past the SLP models, one of the harder and less obvious questions becomes what the actual architecture of the MLP should be and how this affects the performance of the model. This section discusses some of the concerns that the developer should bear in mind.

Back-propagation Algorithm for multi-layer perceptron Models:

The first step is to start with the initialization all weights via sampling from normal distribution.

Second step: Go with input data and proceed to pass data through hidden layers to output layers.

Third step: Count gradient and update these weights.

Forth step: Repeat steps 2 and 3 until the algorithm converges upon tolerable

loss threshold or maximum iterations have been reached.

```
#Generating New Data
x <- as.matrix(seq(-10, 10, length = 100))
```

y <- logistic(x) + rnorm(100, sd = 0.2)

#Plotting Data

plot(x, y)

lines(x, logistic(x), lwd = 10, col = "gray")

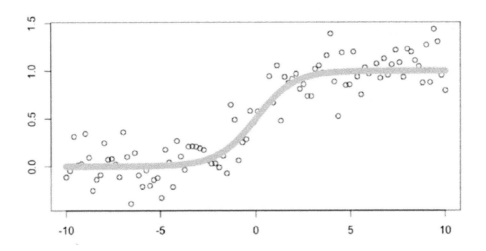

#Loading Required Packages

require(ggplot2)

require(lattice)

require(nnet)

require(pROC)

require(ROCR)

require(monmlp)

#Fitting Model

```
_mlpModel<- monmlp.fit(xx = xz, yx = y, hidden1 = 3,
monotone = 1,
n.ensemble = 15, bag = TRUE)
mlpModel<- monmlp.predict(x = x, weights = mlpModel)
#Plotting predicted value over actual values
for(i in 1:15){
lines(x, attr(mlpModel, "ensemble")[[i]], col = "red")
}
```

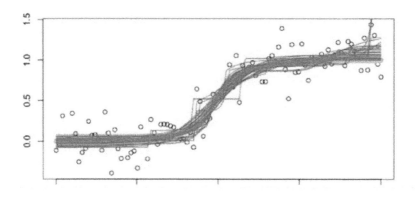

As you can see, there are instances in which the model captures some noise,

evidenced by any deviations from the shape of the logistic function. But all the lines produced are overall a good generalization of the logistic function that underlies the pattern of the data. This is an easy display of the MLP model's ability to handle non-linear functions. This concept also holds true in other practical examples.

Limitations and Considerations for MLP Models

It is a problem if you are using a back-propagation algorithm, when the error is a function of the weights; that convergence upon a global optimal can be hard to solve.

For example, when we are trying to optimize non-linear functions, many

local minima obscure the global minimum. We can therefore be tricked into thinking we've found a model which can effectively solve the problem when in fact we've chosen a solution that doesn't effectively reach the global minimum.

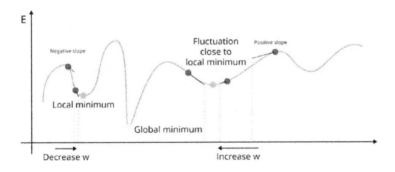

To solve that, the conjugate gradient algorithm is applied.

Conjugate gradient

algorithms differ from the traditional gradient descent method in that the learning rate is adjusted upon every iteration. Many types of conjugate gradient ways have been designed, but all of them have the same underlying motivation to them.

In the context of the MLP network, we're trying to find the weights that minimize the error function. To do this, we move in the direction of steepest descent, but we change the step size in such a way that it minimizes any possible "missteps" in searching for the global optimum. Let's take a simple example where we're trying to solve $Ax = b$

How Many Hidden Layers to Use and How Many Neurons Are in It?

We typically choose to use hidden layers only in the event that data is not linearly separable. Whenever step, heave side, or threshold activation functions are utilized, it is generally advisable to use two hidden layers. With respect to using more than one hidden layer, it's largely unnecessary because the increase in performance from using two or more layers is negligible in most situations. In situations where this may not be the case, experimentation by observing the RMSE or another statistical indicators over the number of hidden layers should be used as a method of deciding.

Often, when adding a layer to a neural network model this will be as simple as editing an argument in a function or, in the case of some deep learning frameworks such as mxnet (featured in later chapters), passing values from a previous layer through an entirely new function.

Thanks to lots of neurons that should be into a given hidden layer, this should be evaluated for with the objective of minimizing the training error. Some suggest that it has to be between the input and output layer size, never more than twice the number of inputs, capturing .70-.90 variance of the initial dataset.

Let's briefly look at the difference between the conjugate gradient training method and traditional gradient descent using the RNSS package in R with the following code:
#Conjugate Gradient Trained NN
conGradMLP<- mlp(x = x, y = y,
size = (2/3)*nrow(x)*2,

maxit = 200,

learnFunc = "SCG")

#Predicted Values

y_h<- predict(conGradMLP, x)

We begin by defining the neural network using the mlp()
function, in which we

specifically denote the learnFunc argument as SCG (scaled
conjugate gradient). We also choose the size parameter (the
number of neurons in a neural network) using the 2/3 rule
mentioned earlier.

Now let's compare the MSE of both the MLP model shown
prior and the one we've just constructed:

MSE for Conjugate Gradient Descent Trained Model:
0.03533956

MSE for Gradient Descent Trained Model: 0.03356279

Although there is only a slight difference in this instance, we
can see that the conjugate gradient method yields a slightly
inferior MSE value than the traditional gradient descent
method in this instance. As such, it would be wise, given this

trend of staying consistent, to pick the gradient descent trained method.

Questions

1. Write the back-propagation algorithm for multi-layer perceptron models.
2. Explain the difference between MLP and SLP.

Chapter 4

Autoencoders, Restricted Boltzmann Machines

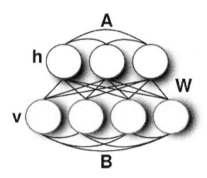

Autoencoders

It's essential to comprehend autoencoders as an arrangement of related algorithms. This idea is known as a feature extractor, as they can figure out how to encode or even to represent information.

The information entered to a Boltzmann-machine would be similar information that we can enter to any machine learning algorithm, however, to make it straightforward, you can accept that on the off chance that it is a M x N matrix every section is a unique component and each row a one of a kind observation of N features. It is an unsupervised learning technique that utilizes back-propagation to figure out how to remake its own sources of information that were inputted.

Created by a great researcher, alongside different specialists, autoencoders address the issue of how to perform back-propagation without expressly advising the Autoencoders what to learn from.

Let us comprehend the structure of the autoencoders and understand that they have two sections: the encoder and the decoder. Let's take an easy and simple case of what we will signify as a n/p/n autoencoder architecture. This architecture is indicated by n, p, m, LV, AB, and XD, where the accompanying are valid:

1. L V and are sets.
2. n and p are positive integers where $0 << p$ n.
3. Let ✏be a function where ✏: . L V p n $\rightarrow$
4. Let ⛀be a function where ⛀: . V L n p $\rightarrow$

Linear Autoencoders vs. Principal Components Analysis (PCA)

The essential focal point of PCA is to locate the linear changes of the original informational index that contain the most fluctuation inside them. In the event that you try to decipher and investigate the original informational collection, we utilize this to accomplish dimensionality reduction, yet I will clarify the relationship it has with linear autoencoders here.

Clearly expressed, PCA is a symmetrical linear change where we look to augment the difference inside every primary part subject to the imperative that every main segment is uncorrelated with each other. Let's characterize y as the accompanying:

$$y \, A \, i \, i = x \, ,$$

Restricted Boltzmann Machines

In the 80s, a gathering of researchers and architects executed this algorithm, which can be portrayed as a kind of a neural system. At the time, it represented a leap forward in the study of deep learning since it was among the primary models to have the capacity to take in the inward portrayals of data and have a capacity to tackle troublesome and difficult issues.

The standard limited Boltzmann machine has a binary value covered up and an unmistakable unit that comprises of a matrix of weights; we connected with the association between a given arrangement of both covered up and noticeable units, and a bias weight.

The non-visible, noticeable, and bias units can be thought of as comparable to those same units that show up in a multilayer perceptron model. Given these, the energy of a setup is expressed as:

$$E(v,h) = -\sum_{i=1}^{N} a_i v_i - \sum_{j=1}^{N} b_j h_j - \sum_{i=1}^{N}\sum_{j=1}^{N} v_i w_{i,j} h_j$$

After you enter everything into the model, each node in the system gets particular values that can be numerically determined. The system is then subjected to various iterations utilizing asynchronous or synchronous updating. After a hard criterion is achieved, the qualities inside the neurons are shown. The fundamental function of these systems is to find the patterns put away in the weight matrix.

While alluding back to the RBM model, the probability conveyances that underlie the information are:

$$P(v,h) = \frac{1}{Z} e^{-E(v,h)}, \ Z = \sum e^{-E(v,h)},$$

$$P(v) = \frac{1}{Z} \sum e^{-E(v,h)}$$

The E (h) is the "exponential" function, and the content is the non-positive estimation of the vitality work that you saw previously.

+

T-+he RBMs and show diagrams have the mutual alternatives. For instance, the initiations from the concealed units are both not reliant, given the actuations from the non-concealed units, so that

$$P(v|h)=\prod_{i=1}^{N}P\big(h_j|v\big), \ P(h|v)=\prod_{j=1}^{N}P\big(h_j|v\big),$$

and the following activation probabilities such as

$$P\big(h_j=1|v\big)=\sigma\bigg(b_i+\sum_{j=1}^{N}w_{i,j}v_i\bigg), \ P\big(v_i=1|h\big)=\sigma\bigg(a_j+\sum_{i=1}^{M}w_{i,j}h_i\bigg),$$

$$\sigma=\frac{1}{1+e^{-k(x-x_0)}}$$

The "a" here is the enactment unit. You can find and discover the estimations of the units of RBMs that can be gotten from a multinomial distribution, while the estimations of the concealed units are gotten from a Bernoulli dissemination.

In the case that we utilize a softmax work for the unmistakable units, you can analyze this function:

$$P\left(v_i^k = 1 \mid h\right) = \frac{exp\left(a_i^k + \sum_{j=1} W_{i,j}^k h_j\right)}{\sum_{k=1}^{K} exp\left(a_i^k + \sum_{j=1} W_{i,j}^k h_j\right)}$$

Contrastive Divergence (CD) Learning

Developed by a great scientist, contrasting divergence (CD) learning is a standard function in the training of restricted Boltzmann machines. This is dependent on the idea of using a Gibbs sampling, run for S steps, where it is initialized with a training example of the training set and yields the sample after S steps.

Created by an extraordinary researcher, contrasting divergence (CD) learning is a standard capacity in the preparation of limited Boltzmann machines. This is subject to utilizing a Gibbs sampling, keep running for S steps, where it is instated with a training case of the preparation set and yields the example after S steps.

It has more extensive applications as a training technique for undirected graph models, however, it's most well-known utilization example is the preparation of RBMs. This can now move us to the definition, and I'll start by characterizing the GD of the log probability:

$$\sum_h p(h|v)\frac{\partial E(v,h)}{\partial w_{i,j}} = \sum_h p(h|v)h_i v_j = \sum_h \prod_{k=1}^{n} p(h_k|v)h_i v_j$$

$$= \sum_{h_i}\sum_{h_{-i}} p(h_i|v)p(h_i|v)h_i v_j$$

$$= \sum_{h_i} p(h_i|v)h_i v_j \sum_{h_{-i}} p(h_{-i}|v) = p(H_i=1|v)v_j$$

$$= sig\left(\sum_{j=1}^{m} w_{i,j}v_j + c_i\right)$$

All things considered, we can state that the log probability is the likelihood of a parameter when it has a value. Already, we characterized the sig () function as the sig () number function, which restores the indication of an input. As should be obvious in the accompanying, you will characterize the GD of the log probability of practice design v with the accompanying condition:

$$\frac{\partial \ln \mathcal{L}(\theta | v)}{\partial w_{i,j}} = -\sum_h p(h|v) \frac{\partial E(v,h)}{\partial w_{i,j}} + \sum_{v,h} p(v,h) \frac{\partial E(v,h)}{\partial w_{i,j}}$$

$$= \sum_{h_i} p(h_i|v) h_i v_j - \sum_v p(v) \sum_h p(h|v) h_i v_j$$

$$= p(H_i = 1|v) v_j - \sum_v p(v) p(H_i = 1|v) v_j$$

The choices of each parameter will be tallied from the working function as respect to the expectations function p (v). In batch learning, you can figure the GD utilizing the total of the practice set.

Still, there are occurrences where it can be figured out in a compelling method to run this estimate over a subset of the training informational set, which we indicate as a small batch. On the off chance that we assess an individual component of the practice set when playing out this estimation, it's known as online learning.

In RBMs, I see that the error as the distinction between the genuine input and the anticipated information, which falls all of a sudden from the earliest starting point of training while advancing. It is proposed that this metric be utilized, yet continue with caution.

The learning algorithm is really improving the KL difference between our practice information and the information created by the Boltzmann machines, and in addition the Gibbs chain's mixing rate. You can state that the remaking error can mostly be little if the mixing rate is likewise little.

Working with the weights inside the RBM increment, normally we watch the mixing rate move inversely. However, a lower mixing rate doesn't generally fundamentally mean a model is better than one in which there is an increased mixing rate.

The weights, like other deep learning models, are beginning to start by values selected without any reason from the general dissemination or other limitless small values. As for the learning rate, similar points with gradient methods must be considered, especially being mindful so as not to pick a learning rate that is excessively bigger or too little.

You can state, a versatile learning rate may cause issues as it will give the appearance that the model is enhancing because of a lower reconstruction error, be that as it may, this may not generally be the situation. It is prescribed that each weight update, for the most part, should be 3 to 10 times the present weights.

Starting hidden biases and weights are ordinarily introduced by choosing them randomly from an ordinary distribution, as is standard working strategy for other neural system models.

Instead of the conventional gradient descent formula, you may utilize another like the momentum method which incrementally influences the speed of the parameter update.

We characterize momentum as the level of the velocity that still exists after a given epoch; we can assume that the velocity of a parameter slows down after some time. On account of that, the momentum method makes the change of the parameters move toward a path that isn't the steepest drop, just like a general gradient method with one main difference – lack of intricacy.

When utilizing the momentum method, it is proposed that the force parameter, α, be set to .5. When it becomes harder to decrease the reconstruction error any further, the momentum ought to be expanded to .9. On the off chance that we see flimsiness in the reconstruction error—ordinarily noted by incidental and incremental increase—we diminish the learning rate by factors of 2 until the point when this event dies down. We characterize the momentum method for changing a parameter as:

$$\Delta\theta_i(t) = v_i(t) = \alpha v_i(t-1) - \epsilon \frac{dE(t)}{d\theta_i}$$

Weight Decay

Weight decay is a phenomenon that can be described as a model of regularization; this includes parameter regularization that can be seen in the ridge regression and/or LASSO. RMBs tend to in the beginning use normal form, which can also be noted as the price of the weights. Subscribers generally use the derivative of the penalty term and then take its product with the learning rate.

This disallows the learning rate from updating the end goal of the function that we are attempting to make more efficient. Weight decay also ensures that overfitting is decreased in a way that the answer that we get does not have units that have uncharacteristically huge weights or weights that keep on going on or off. This also helps in making the mixing rate better, especially with respect to the Gibbs sampling that we attempt, making CD learning more precise. A researcher has also suggested that we should begin a weight with a price of 0.0001.

Sparsity

Lastly, you should remember that a great mode is always one

that has units that cannot be seen and are active only for some time.

Models that have units that are active for only part of the time are simpler and easier to interpret as opposed to models that are populated with a huge amount of active units. We can also get sparsity in our model by specifically pointing out the probability of a unit being on, this can be achieved by using regularization. It will be reflected by q and can be measured by this function:

$$q_{new} = \lambda q_{ild} + (1 - \lambda) q_{current},$$

With respect to the units that are non-visible, the main area of focus is to avoid any kind of overfitting. Truly, we have to use less hidden units instead of using more, especially if the information throughout the observations are likely to be extremely homogeneous.

Furthermore, the only time it is appropriate to use a larger number of hidden units rather than the ordinary amount is if the sparsity goal that we are trying to achieve even remotely happens to fall inside a very small range (or if itself is very small).

Questions

1. What do you know about Restricted Boltzmann Machines?
2. What is weight decay?

Chapter 5

Experimental Design and Heuristics

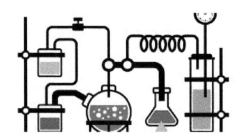

Analysis of Variance (ANOVA)ANOVA is a collection of methods that can be used to observe the variation between different groups of observation inside the information. It is just an extended version of the z and t test, and is the same as regression; we can study the relationship that occurs between the response and explanatory variables. We can also assume that the values we observe within the data are not related to anything else and are identically distributed (IID) normal random variables in which the leftovers are ordinarily dispersed and that the variance is homogenous.

There are numerous ANOVA models, from them a few of the interesting ones are:

One-Way ANOVA

- When you are trying to study the means/averages of three or more sample spaces to each other.

To be more specific, it can be used in the events where the finding is attempted by one variable/factor which has two or more levels.

Two-Way (Multiple-Way) ANOVA

- It's almost the same as the one-way ANOVA, except that this model can be utilized in the cases where the explanatory variables are two or more.

Mixed-Design ANOVA

On the other side of the model that was just described, the mixed-design ANOVA is different the others only in the cases when most of the import factor variables can be analyzed throughout the subjects, and other reasons can be within-subjects variable.

Multivariate ANOVA (MANOVA)

This is the one that is the same as the one-way and two-way ANOVA, the only difference being that it is specifically used to analyze sample means that are multivariate, or if the explanatory variables are two or more in any given information set.

Now that we have familiarized ourselves with the ANOVA models, in the next section we will talk about the different method by which we can measure the results: the F-statistic.

F-Statistic and F-Distribution

Ronald Fisher is the person after whom this method is named. The F-statistic can be found by taking the ratio of two statistical variances. The F-statistic is related to the F-distribution, which is a never ending probability dispersion.

We can see this dispersion as the distribution which is empty of any test statistic for the F-test. Imagine that you have variables A and B so that it happens that they both consist of chi-square distribution, and their extents of freedom are n and d respectively:

$$X = \frac{\frac{A}{n}}{\frac{V}{d}},$$

$$f(x) = \left[\frac{\Gamma\left(\frac{n}{2} + \frac{d}{2}\right)}{\Gamma\left(\frac{n}{2}\right)\Gamma\left(\frac{d}{2}\right)} \right] \left(\frac{n}{d}\right) \left(\frac{\left[\left(\frac{n}{d}\right)x\right]^{\frac{n}{2}-1}}{\left[1 + \left(\frac{n}{d}\right)x\right]^{\frac{n}{2}+\frac{d}{2}}} \right), \quad x \in (0, \infty)$$

If you are now taking a one-method ANOVA and you assume that a set of population will have means that are the same and ordinarily dispersed. You can describe the F-statistic as:

$$F = \frac{\frac{SSE}{k}}{\frac{SSR}{n-k-1}} = \left(\frac{\frac{\sum\left(\hat{Y}_i - \bar{Y}\right)^2}{k}}{\left(\frac{\sum\left(Y_i - \hat{Y}_i\right)^2}{n-k-1}\right)} \right),$$

The k in all of this reflects the extent of freedom, and n can be seen as the amount of n response variables. The null hypothesis explains that any model that is created using an x-intercept and a model that occurs by the user creates results that cannot be differentiated (inside any given confidence interval).

The other hypothesis explains that the model which is created by the reader will be exponentially more efficient than a model that only has the x intercept. Just like when you are checking any other measure of statistical importance, this can be determined on the basis of the threshold that you wish to set. (90% level of confidence, 95% level of confidence, and so on).

We can look at another example to understand and apply the concept that we have just learned. Just in this example, we will be utilizing the iris data set:

```
#Loading Data
data("iris")
#Simple ANOVA
#Toy Example Using Iris Data as Y
y <- iris[, 1]
x <- seq(1, length(y), 1)
plot(y)
```

The information collected will be used to make responses and/or explanatory variables in the accompanying examinations. In the event that you recollect from the past illustration, we take the primary column of the iris information index (reflecting to the sepal length of every observation) and make this explanatory variable.

Now, before we perform a one-way ANOVA, we should prove the assumptions important to fit information to a linear model. You will begin working by visually assessing your information, as in this figure:

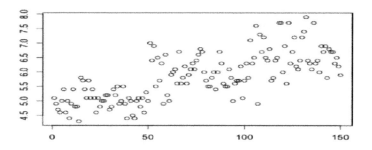

Promptly, we see that the information is genuinely linear in its appearance, highlighting a positive slope. It is a vital factor, yet you will burrow further to guarantee that whatever remains of our presumptions are fulfilled. In this case, we'll look at plotting the residuals of a fitted model. By residuals, I mean the amount left from the rest of the real value minus the value anticipated by the model. You ought to vigorously use residual analysis when working with linear models, yet additionally by and large, since they give incredible visual understanding into how well a specific model functions, and the appearance of the data plot(glm(y~x)).

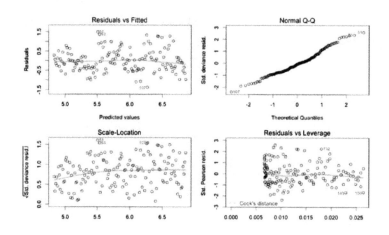

Note the chart in the upper right-hand corner of the four showed in the above figure. This is a quantile plot, which viably shows how much the dispersion of the residuals are ordinary. When intently assessing the plot, you can see that a lot of the information will lie on the dotted 45-degree angle line, which is the marker of regularity in the information.

Nonetheless—and as is normally the case—you can see that the last parts have a tendency to marginally lift over this line.

It's exceptionally import to see that quite often, the information we will qualify as being regularly disseminated will display comparable examples. In the genuine example, most information has a tendency to be near to regular distribution when we have enough of it, however, it's impossible that it will be flawlessly, typically dispersed.

In that capacity, we acknowledge that the information is regularly disseminated and move onto proving the rest of the assumptions. At the point when the information is typically distributed, it can be fit into a linear model and in this manner, we can sensibly find the values inside the scope of the x variable.

Since we additionally require that errors show consistent variance, so how about we direct our concentration toward the plot in the upper left-hand corner. Note that a plot with an x-axis signifies the value that the regression yielded and a y-axis denotes the residual value. The horizontal line through the focal point of the plot reflects the area where the fitted value is equivalent to the genuine value, or where observations have residual that is 0.

While alluding particularly to our information, we can see that as a rule, the state of the residuals plotted is by all accounts steady from the left to the right side of the plot. All things considered, we would note that the residuals do in truth display steady variance.

If not, we would see that there would be unmistakable patterns in the state of the dissipated plot that would either turn out to be more overstated or less misrepresented from the left to the right side of the plot. Generally, we consider an observation as being especially important if its Cook's distance value is more noteworthy than 1 or if its distance value is more noteworthy than $4/n$.

Which limit to utilize is at last up to you, yet clearly this will rely upon the case, and it is worth reviewing on an experimental basis which furnishes a dataset with more or less exceptions, and how that would influence your ultimate objective.

In the event that, for instance, the motivation behind a test is anomaly recognition, it may be absurd to decrease the limit so more noise in the dataset is qualified as a signal. While alluding back to our particular plot, we can see that a lot of information points are being hailed as having considerable influence. You ought to recall that as we push ahead with our model decision.

While evaluating every one of the plots in the data collection, we can unhesitatingly say that in spite of the fact that there are exceptions, and our presumptions aren't met flawlessly, the strength of OLS regression enables these slight deviations to be dealt with. All things considered, it's sensible to pick OLS regression as a model for this task, and thus ANOVA will yield statistically noteworthy outcomes.

Similarly as when we utilize the summary function on a GLM protest, we are given a measure of its statistical noteworthiness. Rather than a Z-score, we're given a F-score from the idea we discussed preceding this illustration and its relative P-score.

In this occurrence, we can state with 99% surety that the outcomes we dismiss is the null hypothesis. Accordingly, this model is an altogether preferred fit over an intercept-only model, and consequently we can be more certain about its outcomes.

Be that as it may, suppose we want to compare multiple fitted models. All things considered, how about we assess what happens when we incorporate in excess of one variable and concentrate on the interaction among them. As should be obvious in the code, I utilize the second and third columns as explanatory variables in this model.

When fitting our model, we take the product of both the explanatory variables. When carrying out the code, we can see the following result:

```
#Mixed Design Anova
x1 <- iris[,2]
x2 <- iris[,3]
mixedAOV<- aov(y ~ x1*x2)
summary(mixedAOV)
```

Df Sum Sq Mean Sq F value	Pr(>F)			
x1 x2 x1:x2 Residuals	1	1.41	1.41 84.43 0.35 0.11	12.9 0.000447 *** 771.4 < 2e-16 *** 3.2 0.075712 .
1 84.43				
1	0.35			
146 15.98				

The residuals we have are notably smaller, and all the other variables have a lot of statistical significance at least with a 90% confidence interval. Let's carry out this code and then visually differentiate between the two models:

```
par(mfrow = c(2,2))
```

```
plot(glm(y ~ x1*x2))
dev.off()
```

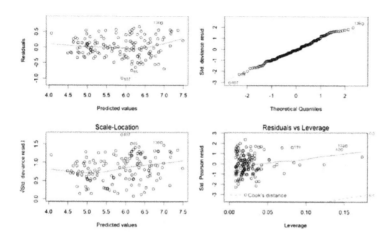

Fisher's Principles

Ronald Fisher is one of the most noteworthy statisticians to have ever lived on this planet. He explained what the principle for experimental design is and he is known everywhere because of it. These are the various explanations of his principle, along with it there is also some regular advice on how you want to use these principles:

1. *Statement of Experiment*: You should out rightly tell the exact things that led to the experiment, also make sure that you clearly give an overview of the steps that will be involved in

the experiment on a very high level. Generally speaking, the rule regarding the introduction is that it should have a high-level review of the topic, and every section of it should explain some other component in extreme detail, going from the starting of the experiment to the end in a logical progression.

2. *Interpretation and its Reasoned Basis:* From the starting, it's sensible to give what you may hope to be the sensible results. You should express the results that you feel must be considered, however, understand that giving an unending rundown of results for those to whom you answer to isn't probably going to be extremely useful. In addition, while talking about all the conceivable results, do as such in a way that gives noteworthy bits of knowledge to those perusing your examination. Research that gives significant bits of knowledge leaves more space for misapplication.

3. *The Test of Significance:* with regards to assessing machine learning and profound learning arrangements, a basic recommendation is to bootstrap the test insights used to assess a given model. It's sensible to accept that in the event that you draw enough test measurements over a sufficiently long time, the information will be ordinarily distributed. Starting here, a Z-test can be performed to decide the sensible level of factual confidence that one has in the model.

4. The Null Hypothesis: This theory should express that the outcomes indicated have no value or significance, and any deviation between testing populaces is because of some superfluous error, for example, wrong sampling or deviations from legitimate experimental rules. This must be a segment of all statistical testing.

5. Randomization: The Physical Basis of the Validity of the Test: When playing out a test, the outcomes that are achieved ought to be performed in a way that the result was not biased. Now and again, this may require randomized observations of information to expel any intuitive or inherent predispositions that exists in the demonstrating of the experiment that would prompt a few outcomes.

6. Statistical Replication: The outcomes achieved from a test must be replicable. Results that are absurd given the requirements inherent to the information collection and condition in which we hope to watch such an event are not as important as results that are replicable.

7. Blocking: The procedure by which diverse experimental gatherings are compartmentalized so diverse varieties and inclinations are lessened or even kept totally from influencing the aftereffects of an examination.

Plackett-Burman Designs

The Plackett-Burman design was created by Robin Plackett and J.P. Burman in the 1940s. Plackett-Burman designs are a way of finding out the quantifiable dependence of explanatory variables that we like to call factors in this case, in which factor has L levels. Overall, the end goal is to reduce the variance of the estimates of dependencies by utilizing a small number of experiments.

If you want to achieve this, an experimental design is picked so that every combination that is made from any pair of factors is shown equally throughout every run that we carry out as an experiment.

The Plackett-Burman design need a few number of experiments, to be more specific – it has to be a multiple up until 36 from 4, and the design is supposed to have a certain number of sample that can be studied up to k parameters, where $k = N - 1$. In the event that $L = 2$, we use an orthogonal matrix inside which every element is either -1 or 1. You can also call this matrix a Hadamard matrix.

This methods is great if you want to find out the main impact of divers factors on the response variable, so that we can get rid of the factors that seem like they have a little or no impact. Plackett and Burman have themselves given detailed designs for L equaling 3, 4, 5 and 7.

If we now look at the matrix, which visually shows a Burman design. When executing this design of experiments (DOE), you should write down the right row as the starting row of the design table. In this circumstance, we start with a +, -, +, -, +, +. This is just a permutation of the sequence that shows in each row, which reflects a treatment combination. You can imagine that a treatment combination is a special combination of a future set. The second row then appears if you shift sequence in the row before towards the right by one column. The problem will now be replicated for all the rows that were leftover. The row, in the end, shows all the non-positive elements.

| | Factors | | | | | | |
Treatment Combinations	A	B	C	D	E	F	G
1	+	-	-	+	-	+	+
2	+	+	-	-	+	-	+
3	+	+	+	-	-	+	-
4	-	+	+	+	-	-	+
5	+	-	+	+	+	-	-
6	-	+	-	+	+	+	-
7	-	-	+	-	+	+	+
8	-	-	-	-	-	-	-

A/B Testing

When planning applications, sites, or dashboard applications, it's valuable to decide the impact that adjustments in specific functionalities have on the item. We can envision, for instance, that an engineer is endeavoring to decide with some measurable certainty whether the usage of another element has affected procuring new clients. For such circumstances, it's suggested that the individual utilize something known as A/B testing. Comprehensively, A/B testing alludes to the statistical theory testing method used to analyze two datasets in comparison with each other, a control gathering, and a test aggregate - A and B. We can likewise change the test so we can test A and have numerous extra control tests.

Questions

1. Explain A/B Testing in your own words.

2. What is the Plackett-Burman design?

Reference Page

- **Introduction to Deep Learning Using R** - Taweh Beysolow